Sea Snails on a Black Chow's Tongue

OR, A CASTAWAY'S POEMS IN A BOTTLE

Sea Snails on a Black Chow's Tongue

OR, A CASTAWAY'S POEMS IN A BOTTLE

KEITH HARVEY

iUniverse, Inc.
New York   Bloomington

iUniverse books may be ordered through booksellers or by contacting:

iUniverse
1663 Liberty Drive
Bloomington, IN 47403
www.iuniverse.com
1-800-Authors (1-800-288-4677)

Because of the dynamic nature of the Internet, any Web addresses or links contained in this book may have changed since publication and may no longer be valid. The views expressed in this work are solely those of the author and do not necessarily reflect the views of the publisher, and the publisher hereby disclaims any responsibility for them.

ISBN: 978-1-4401-7885-6 (sc)
ISBN: 978-1-4401-7887-0 (dj)
ISBN: 978-1-4401-7886-3 (ebook)

Library of Congress Control Number: 2009937566

Printed in the United States of America

iUniverse rev. date: 10/05/09

D'où venons nous? Que sommes nous? Où allons nous?

Paul Gauguin

Contents

PREFACE

This collection of poems follows two earlier books in theme and style: *Petroglyphs* and *Cave Gossip*. *Cave Gossip* is a novel, and *Petrogyphs* is my first collection of poems. The themes of both works are the same: humanity's need to create myths to explain and shield itself from chaotic and finite existence. From that generality, I move to the specific and the subjective.

In this work, I continue the themes of myth and myth-making and elaborate on some of my own private and somewhat obsessive images and myths. For a long time, maybe thirty years, I have imagined the journey of the snail is similar to our journey. Our poems, stories, ideologies, religious beliefs, and social structures are shells that protect us from the chaotic outside—nature. The snail has a finite journey, which in my observation, is usually from the yard to the flowerbed. Its journey can be analogized to our birth, life, and death. This life, this journey, is the hero's way.

I also believe we make our journey alone. We are castaways in a savage world, and our ancestors in myth are sailors like Ulysses, Jonah, Robinson Crusoe, the Swiss Family Robinson, the colonists at Jamestown, the French at Quebec in the sixteenth century, and Paul Gauguin. Through our voyages, wrecks, drownings, and resurrections, we change alchemically and become something else—we walk on our heads and speak in tongues.

This book is dedicated to my father, who loves black chows and who has walked the warrior's way.

But he is not the only father in this book. My intellectual fathers are Hermes, Homer, Socrates, Nietzsche, Heidegger, Paul Celan, Wallace Stevens, Dr. John Dee, William Shakespeare, Ted Hughes, Dali, Breton, Rimbaud, Franz Kafka, Thomas Mann, the translators of the King James Version of the Bible, Carl Jung, Sigmund Freud, and every man or woman who climbed onto the wooden and splintered deck of a ship bound for the New World or waited in an upper room for the *heilige Geist* to descend on fiery wings.

I also want to thank Ms. SarahA O'Leary in Portsmouth, England, who read every word in the manuscript and provided a sweet heigh-ho through the virtual net, and Dr. Ronald Schenk, who knows a thing or two about sunken quests and pregnant fish.

DEDICATION

Gene Allen Harvey

Liminal State

The other Oyle is prest out
of the dried Cocus, which is called Copra

Deep down
on the lower level,
beneath the sea-green
breakers, we walk on our head.

At night we dream
of parakeets in palms,
as brown-bronze women
dance on yellow sand.

Yesterday we piloted
a silver schooner
through the archipelago
and traded Gaugins
for copra.

We serve the sea-spider;
we breathe through gills.

Tomorrow we hide
in a coral niche
and count starfish
with tattooed eyes.

Rimbaud's Color Wheel

The center-word
does not hold
its color-sounds
alone

they swirl
within the sun-threads
first black then white
green then blue

until the red appears
so red that we see
gold

the danger
though is that blue
bruises black
and begins to turn
again

Seven Steps in Sense Sequence Plus Two

we have
explored
the primal word
and magic numbers
but do not forget
the sense of color

Wittgenstein and Goethe
knew its worth
and the cabalists
its symbol

expect now
both number
and color
when we do
what we do

to make
or unmake
poetry of
nine levels
or three squared

The Futility of Stratagems

gardens grow wild
within the squared
circle
of big mind

throughout its spheres
nature orders
chaotic growth

and cosmic mechanics
whirl metallic wheels
as daffodils drip
drops of oily dew
onto blind eyes

Order in the Time of Ramses

twelve hours of day
balance against twelve of night

the rule writ
on papyrus

work in light
sleep at twilight

but to be safe
light the oil lamp
at dusk
to drive
daemons away

Abstraction

Rousseau paints green
on the jungle canvas

his yellow parrots
parade on jagged limbs
where jaguars sleep
jade in verdant shadows

mottled leaves dry
from an afternoon rain
and sun-threads reign
over jaundiced puddles

where parrots drink
and the Paraclete
sleeps shuttered
in the jaguar's keep

Tiny Bats

hang like green grapes
beneath Congress Street Bridge

at dusk
they drop

gulp air
and jettison
guano

their numbers
paint the sky
black

they spread
like treacle
through ebony
night

on Bollingen Island
fox bats
fall free
under ebon
limbs

at dusk
they eat
pomegranates
with simian hands

at dawn they sleep
suspended

swaying
in sour wind

Process D'or

line ends
your breath

but to breathe
signifies
a four-fold
sign
of green

so exit
timeless
and dream
blue

but do not fall
or fail
for a bruise
re-boots
black

Chows Bark Primal Words

to the two Ws—Walt and Wallace

they sing the lyric of the lower man

as black-tongued chows they bark
primordial words like familial hounds

their harried language howls to the languid
lovers of the lower level and like
Puritans in their log cabins they pray
for the patriarch's provision of profit

owls observe their shadowed orbs
beneath the New England woods
and doves huddle in their hutch
cooing to the sweet squabs
that squeak tomorrow's sun

their fresh feathers fray
throughout the night's somber
embrace and the moon's frigid light

at dawn a pigeon carries a message
to the sun-knitted in angelic sun-threads

the primal word images God
through the lower ones
and incarnates the quotidian
on parchment

receiving the message on winged tongues
the Pilgrims pray for transcendence
but the elect find their wealth
in the moldering soil of the worms

the worms wiggle on hooks of desire
the chow tongues once blackened catch fire

Primal Patriarch

he appeared
then her

his son died
murdered by his brother

eventually he died
from her
to the earth

it was his end
but not the end

the hierarchy
arose
from a cut
pruned
from a yellow rose

now he ascends
and descends
toward transcendence

The Fact of the Doing Thing

the job
that works
us
is not
the one
we waited
for in fact
the work
we do
is not
the one
we dreamed
of nor trained
for nor interviewed
with nor even
wanted
instead we do
what we do
because we
can do
no other
thing

Poet

He sat and read
his primal poems
on a wooden stool
carved from pine.
His lips purpled
as he scanned
primordial words
and his tongue
shadowed
like a chow's.

Mug's Game

the mug's game has no rules

only a prescription

grind dragon bone
into powder
and drink it in green tea

purple visions may appear
and sear
the mind's eye
with images so abstract
the tiger lily
will bloom red

then yellow light
will burst bright
from the book's binding
and lean lines
will form left
before marching
down blanched
pages of Set's papyrus

Fingerprints

for every touch a print is made
not on water but on clay
for every breath upon a leaf
a bit of moisture remains
for every sight an image lingers
and for every sigh an ache
for each encounter with an Angel
one broken limps away

Method

The chow barks
a snail's portrait

its threefold
sign
triples one round
shell

to read its whorl
is to hear a star gasp

a frozen breath inward

to hear the whorl
is to read a sea-green sea

Sargasso
into a blue
Geist

Sulphur

sulphur
the driest salt
sprinkles
from her fevered brain

her projection
is her protection

but it makes
no sense
because sulphur
as salt
possesses savor
only after fault

Freud's Pillow or Lot's Lot

soaked

in her juices
for six decades

he now awaits
her second nonage
to air his fate
and faults

maybe chalk
from Dover cliffs
is his place
to crumble
into white waves

but before the stone
hardens into sulphur
and flakes into salt

he looks back
and sees flames
engulf city walls

and salamanders
dance in red

cloaked

Northwest Passage

to Ms. O'Leary

Doctor John Dee
read four thousand books
and spoke
to Annaël
in tongues.

She was his muse
and Spenser's virgin queen.

Together they scried
a darkened way
to a manifest
destiny.

Through chartered
companies
and bartered ships
they struggled
beneath sea-green
ice
and beached
one fateful day
as castaways
in auriferous
Cathay.

Reading John Dee in the Bath

the primal word
reacts
to expansion

emotional flutters
within my ear

a buzzing
of silk wings

and muttering
of a gibbering ghost

a *précis* of
John Dee

proceeds
to the next
numen
perhaps Bes

therefore Lull
lull me
into an alphabetical
mysticism

count ten
on my fingers
and label them
B to K

Anecdote of the Garden

Krazy Kat's fur is black
like the bruised wing of a crow.

Firecat is red
like the speckled eye
of a peacock's feather.

Krazy Kat appeared first,
like Abel, in the world.

Firecat will arrive later,
the last one before the end.

Firecat and Krazy Kat share
the silky sand of his garden.

Krazy Kat slumbers in the shrubs
in the doomed darkness of dusk,
while Firecat dozes on the grate.

Another mediates the in-between;
Snowcat purrs under the red rushes
beyond the bed of purple irises.

Snowcat loves Krazy Kat and Firecat.

Snowcat exists in perpetual winter;
she is the queen of snow
that blows from ether.

Snowcat cannot purr; her throat
is blocked; the glottal stop
is wrecked. Instead, she listens
while Firecat and Krazy Kat sing
a stone-song
trending toward harmony.

The Black Chow

The black chow sleeps
against the door;
her heavy body an impediment
against entering or exiting.
She is a companion
that cannot be left.
Sometimes he throws
a message in a bottle
into the yard
and she springs
away with a cough.
Her weighted soul
splits the air
and her paws
pounce on the prize.
Freed, he slips
from the house,
sacrificing a message
unread. Now chewed
and wet she deposits
it on the stoop
before she settles
like Cerberus
to guard
a captive
who has fled.

A Snail's Tale

A snail on a mirror,
smuggled onto a Russian truck,
one snowy night passes
through the American lines.
That morning it had been a Communist;
by nightfall, it crawled from the polished glass
onto a silk tablecloth in Salzburg,
speaking German and telling a strange tale.
It said, "There are two snails:
the one that speaks here to you
and the other, my twin, that lives
on the other side of the projection.
In that alternate world of thrown light,
my double slithers on slime
along a razor's edge of time
that flows in reverse toward Romania,
where snow buries frigid bodies
crumpled on the side of a ditch,
their eyes perfect calcified shells."

Paul at the Brasserie Lipp

Paul arrived at Brasserie Lipp around 18:30, about thirty minutes before his agreed meeting with Günter.

As the maître d' seated him in one of the banquettes in the entrance, cold rain drizzled down on the gray sidewalks, driving the tourists back to their hotels. He smiled wryly because he didn't like tourists, especially American tourists; their congregating in front of the café to soak up the remaining DNA of the lost generation somehow offended him.

Paul was not immune to the allure of past writers' haunts nor absorbing their DNA. That was why he was at the Lipp rather than some more modest café in his neighborhood. Perhaps that was the real reason why he looked down on the tourists huddling beneath the awning, rain dripping off their noses, waiting for a table that the haughty maître'd may or may not grant them, because he knew he was not much different from them. The only difference, he rationalized, was that he had published a handful of poems in Germany. Somehow that legitimized him, whereas these others were simply that—the others.

As he waited for Günter, he extracted a moleskin notebook from the inside pocket of his tweed jacket and a Pelikan fountain pen he bought in a shop in the center of Frankfurt. He was working on something he believed might be important: a metaphysical conceit he thought of while reading *Robinson Crusoe* by Daniel Defoe and the poetry of Emily Dickinson. He summarized the conceit easily and succinctly: poetry is a message in a bottle, cast into the sea by the poet, to float alone and find its own fate.

Of course, like every conceit, he built upon it and refined it. He even imagined writing a whole series of poems about a shipwrecked and his struggle to live within the confines of a deserted island.

In fact, this morning while shaving he thought of a corollary image, which he thought opened up a new avenue of philosophical development, an avenue which he wanted to discuss with Günter. Suppose a young, idealistic shipwreck throws a bottle into the sea and then, over the years, forgets about it. He goes about his work on the island, doing everything he can to survive. Years later, he is walking on the beach at dusk, when he sees a glint in the sand. He hurries to it and digs it out with his staff. He uncovers a blue-green glass bottle. He examines it and discovers its mouth is sealed with beeswax; he peels the seal back with his long yellow nails and extracts a piece of rolled bark. On the bark he reads a message in smoky charcoal: "I sailed on the HMS *Manifest Destiny* in 1952. The ship sank in the China Sea; all hands were lost except me. Shipwrecked."

The man is startled. He pities the poor man, who, so many years ago, became shipwrecked at the same time as he. A man just like him cast a message into the world, but unfortunately, his message landed on another deserted island. He wonders if he still lives, and then it dawns on him that he is the shipwrecked. With this realization, his hope crumbles and he begins to sob; tears stream down his face. He is alone and the message in the bottle has "unconcealed" his condition in the world. He is a shipwrecked on a deserted island. The sea surrounds him and marks his boundaries. The sky forms his roof and he is mortal, fated to die alone. The help he waited for will not come. With the truth now revealed, he returns to his life on the island, where he dwells.

Günter Arrives Before the Flood

The rain stopped for a minute or two, and the sun seeped through a break in the clouds to illuminate a slice of the pavement in front of the Brasserie Lipp. Paul experienced a glint of light in the corner of his left eye and raised his head from his notebook to glimpse a momentary illumination in the street. Then, thunder rumbled, shaking the foundation of the old building, and the rain returned in iron sheets.

Before returning to his notes on the shipwrecked, Paul recognized a short figure in a wrinkled beige raincoat running across the wide boulevard. The man, with a large pipe clenched between his teeth, dodged cars and jumped puddles, heading inexorably toward the entrance of the Lipp. *It was Günter, late as usual,* he thought, *running to catch up with a deadline he had already missed.*

Günter stopped outside the restaurant, underneath its awnings, and peeled off his wet coat. He shook it several times before he folded it over his left arm. He faced the glass door, and Paul watched as Günter's dark eyes blinked, owl-like, twice behind black horn-rimmed spectacles. The well-lit Lipp and the dark rain-soaked night created a mirror out of the front door, and Paul knew Günter could not see into the restaurant. Instead, he stood before the mirror and prepared himself for his late entrance. Gazing at his image, he ran a fat hand through his thick black hair, removed his wooden pipe, and deposited it into the right-hand pocket of his gray suit. Besides the crumpled suit, Günter wore a pale blue shirt, unbuttoned at the collar, gold cufflinks, and scuffed brown shoes. For finishing touches, he rubbed his left hand over his thick Nietzsche-like mustache and pulled the suit forward at the lapels, as if to make room for his bullish neck and shoulders.

Once inside, the maître'd moved forward, his hand outstretched, as if Hemingway himself had entered the room. He took Günter's coat and pulled out the banquette table to allow him to edge onto Paul's left. The two now sat like an old couple, ensconced in their place of honor, near the door. The placement was significant to all cognoscenti; the two mattered. Their place had been earned. The management placed them to see and be seen.

"May I have a towel, Maurice?" asked Günter in his heavily accented French.

The maître'd snapped a finger, and a middle-aged waiter with thinning hair dyed coal-black rushed forward with a linen towel. Günter rubbed his head down roughly and then asked for Paul's comb. He pulled the thick hair back in several sharp movements. Paul noted his hands were stained black and yellow from ink and nicotine.

"Your hands look as if you have been writing," Paul said in German.

"I have. But not just writing, though. I am producing a baby, a monstrous baby. It's something different from anything else I have written."

The waiter reappeared and asked if they wanted an aperitif.

Günter said, slapping his meaty hands together, "Let's have two Kir Royales. I feel like celebrating the head-birth of my baby."

Snail Silence

The order within him
was so black
he absorbed the sun's rays.
Like moths, bright auras
fluttered toward his darkness
until he could no longer
stand the weight
of their anxious
pushing.
Finally, in despair
he cried out to the snail
that passed beneath him,
sliding on its silver thread:
"Why do they press against me so?
"What have I done to deserve
such dreadful desire?"

Life on the Under Leaf

They emerge from darkness
crawling across the cement
on the way to the garden.
They find their way to the under leaf,
where they sleep through the day
to appear at dusk, to work
their way back to the yard
and the trees. Not once
do they repeat their mathematical
purpose nor speak of their twin
that fades into dark history,
nor do they lecture
on verticality
or the ultimate fate
that awaits the horizon.

Early Snails

The book-troll awakes at five.
Morning frost stained
its windows satin,
as it stood and stared
at the seamless threads
of silver crisscrossing
the sidewalk's gray cement.
It whispered:
"they crossed in the night."
It feared the early snails
who could not decipher
one cellulose
molecule from another.
They chewed relentlessly
on leafy blades and papyrus,
leaving stains and holes
as reminders of their hunger.

The Worms

The snails slumber
in the shade
of the rose leaf,
while the worms
below
churn black soil
like the steel
propeller
of a gray cruiser
furrows
green waves
in the southern sea.

Forget La Giaconda

hierarchy of category
begins with alpha's breath

branches off the knowing tree
and tunnels through worm mold

the rose is the snail's end
a breathless line that connects
old Adam to the castaway

categories incarnate
as each initiate contributes
a thread to the maker's lace

so all the Vermeers wait
with frail facticity

to prove omega's line
ends with lace's last design

Return

after each blow
the worm returns
to its rose
to spin silk
for lace
she makes
under the window

Night-soil

The night-soil
of Darwin's
worms
is saltier
than Persian
caviar;
whereas,
Rumi's poetry
swallows
smoother
than a Gulf
oyster
in November.

Archipelago

The castaway sails between the northern islands
and mines a frozen continent with his art
like the earthworm mulls mold in Darwin's garden.

Oskar as Athena; Günter as Zeus

The two sipped their aperitifs; one gazed outward, while the other turned inward. Günter noted a tall, thin woman with dyed blonde hair and red lips entering the brasserie with a short rotund man wearing a black suit, black tie, and a white shirt. His thinning hair was pulled back and shining from pomade and reflected light. She placed a manicured hand on his round shoulders and pouted. Her nails glimmered red against his gray skin, and Günter thought of Athena springing forth from Zeus's head. Her imagined armor gleamed in the light of the Lipp, and he sighed, wishing for her attention. He decided to use her in his novel that was percolating to the surface of his conscious mind. He imagined sitting at his typewriter, tapping the scene out beneath the single electric light that hung from his dingy ceiling on the Rue d'Italie. He prayed for the gods of modernism to aid him in his creation.

Paul did not notice the woman; instead, he reflected on the phrase "head-birth." His black eyes glazed over as he turned his vision inward, tracing the roots of the expression, seeking the source of the myth of the birth of the parthenogenic goddess. He immediately thought of Hermes as midwife and imagined Athena, as a reincarnation of Neith, the Egyptian goddess of war, who nursed a crocodile at her breast. Paul was a master of slow-reading and metaphors. Already his mind hopped from stone to stone of the mephitic scree of archaic images that lay submerged in his memory. Already, he was cataloging images to produce a poem of disparate associations. He etched crocodiles and ankhs, goddesses and shields, into a fabric of metaphors to express his vision of being. He sank deeper, looking for original images in the ooze of the Nile. He scraped his poem onto papyrus; he employed hieroglyphs to strike the flint. Embers and sparks flew in the summer night, and mosquitoes buzzed through the marshes.

White Bears Red Snakes

white bears on white
snow and blue ice

hunger for black
seals with black eyes

sleeping
on green ice
and white snow

when
ice melts
islands appear
and floes
flow

downstream

between the rifts
of the archipelago

south toward ship
lanes where steam
bellows and screws
torque toward green
land and brown land

in the west

green-blue parrots
shriek in dark jungles
where snakes
entwine
between black
limbs
that shed
red skin

Loon

we searched for bears
but we find a loon
on a purple lake
beneath the larches
swimming alone
dominating the surface
diving deeply

his heavy bones
take him down
as he searches
for silver trout
caught between sky and bottom
delving deeper into darker depths
a mediator of the above
and the below

an aquatic miner.

Readers

he writes a poem
she reads his poem
it is not his poem
it is another thing
her poem

she writes a poem
he reads her poem
it is not her poem
it is a new thing
his poem

they write
they read
the message is not their message
the bottle is not their bottle
it is a found thing
a new thing
the lost thing
the bottle

Beckett Beckons

curtain call
and we take
to the boards

we play Beckett
in the round
and we wait

we wait for lights
and applause

we wait
for roses
and cheering
crowds

we wait
for Beckett
on his deepest ground

as we play the round

56

For his birthday, she gifted
him with a raven fetish,
which, when held,
ensorcelled him
in a shadow
of elder thoughts.
Its shadow spread
and draped
across his shoulders
like Balzac's cloak
cast in bronze
by Rodin,
the French mage.

Wolfgirls Dance Under June's Moon

Caesar nominates
the lion month

its blonde
rays retain
the sun's
son
within a jar
sealed
with beeswax

it contains
oyster beds
marinated in Mexican
brine

groves of palms
spitting purple dates

and their astral
love preserved
during the white nights
of die Deutsche Zeit

but finally
it is time
to spike the seal
and shuck
the shells

blue
he refrains
from flight

and howls
beneath June's
green moon

GI Home 1968

to Harold and Gene

at first light
fog fragments woods
as three men
find the green clearing

they survey
the square
and stake
stakes
into sallow
soil

they twist
twine
around pine
posts
as a preamble

they shovel
sleep-sand
with sharpened
spades

and
measure
flat feet
with fours
and twos

in this rite
they found
foundations
with first
steps

and slay
snakes
with Parsifal's
spear

Hunger

He yearned to be seen;
she hungered to be read.
It was as simple as that.
He published a little magazine;
she wrote sinister poems.
It was as simple as that.
He was twenty-two and lonely;
she was eighteen and sly.
It was as simple as that.
She became pregnant
and killed herself.
He lived a long life
in her shadow.
It was as simple as that.

Tick-Tock

to SarahA.

the real
you deal
is not here

the real
I see
in my liminal
state
is not
your here

here I hear the deaf
and feel the blind

you feel the deaf
and hear the blind

your here
is there

however
our worlds
are there
in the big mind

the singular mind
revolves like a silver
cog
within a brass wheel

guided by the north star
it turns

tick-tock, spin-spin
spin-spin, tick-tock

White Worm

Dwelling in the black,
the white worm called
out: some say white
orders, while chaos'
shadow destroys.
But the circumference
soon centers
that *noir*ish truth.
The worm blanched
by the dark
is no more stable
than a crease
of light
over a lake
on a summer night
or a pursed
lip over her ear.

Haiku-eins

To Paula
silent spring-snow gifts
grass sprinkled with pear petals
and doves in silk drifts

Haiku-zwei

in big mind's wide rink
skaters skate in trim circles
that happily link

My Stylistic Choice

monotones
drone in a gallery

hushed whispers
buzz about without adjectives
and then a laugh

a canvas
seasoned gray
with a violent
splash
of red
hangs
on a wall
painted
eggshell

a dour Dutch
portrait
of a bowl
of brown eggs
two dead fowl
a tumbled glass
of ruby port

and a Burgermeister's
daughter shedding
a gelid tear
poised
on her blue-green
cheek

Stone Measures

poetry sleeps within the stone
while the stone measures the line

the act on board is made
and the doing
done and now alone

like a castaway
the line moves on
as does the raft
as does the bottle
all three bobbing
up and down, then sink
as the horizon shrinks
and seagulls squeal

we remember it
but we cannot recall it

Quarry

to Anschel

my role was ordained

I dig stones
they cement

they are masons
and their measures
are exact

they build
pyramids

each rock
locks
inextricably
to another

Core

we descend
father and son
to the center

our iron picks
sparking
as we strike
red rock

redness
reddens
our blushing
cheeks

flames
flare

and we
are one

at last

Milieu

this experience constitutes a world

the crystal sand in the stained
box
dwells within the snail's memory
of the castaway
who walked on his head

shipwrecked
yet again in the space
between the quietude of play
and the quotidian
worm mold, he scribbles
on Egyptian papyrus
an anecdote of a black
chow
that fetches an artifact
of glued feathers
and glittering leviathan bones

Inked Clay

Silence elevates hermetic supplicants
on feast days and summer solstice.
From dreams they dance
on darkened feet across scree
to the daemon's dire door.
Silver shamans blow rams' horns
to succor the winged spirit.
They present him glazed pots
reddened with tattooed sigils,
signifying the poet's primordial words.
He says:
Doing writ, heralds done.
They repeat it
on percussive sand
burned green into glass.
They seal it
like preserves;
the wide mouth of the mason jar
covered with mother's cheesecloth.

Paraclytus

The poem sags
from definition.
It is invisible
to all but the unseen,
who are only seen
by the invisible;
heard only
because
winged tongues
sometimes scratch
then erase
inked messages.

Friday

I in-dwell within the sea-spider's niche.
Black and spindly, she spreads eight legs
into the nether reach of our aquatic strangeness.
Together we fall toward the star's reach
and embrace beneath the comet's tail.
Together we shuffle on our heads;
our feet slide against the surface's tide.
Anemone and starfish shape our single scar;
the remnant of saturnalian incrustation.

Die Welt

The world
like bread
is made fresh
each day.
Unleavened
it lasts
no longer
than memory.
Seasoned
with reason
it blackens
and crumbles.

Therapy

The point is a whole
and contains no points.
A line is a series of points.
Two points and a line begins.
We sat, two points,
each week
for twelve years
talking. We formed
two lines at right angles,
an analyst and an analysand.
Lines have no breath;
they sigh breathless.
from their silence.
Worlds form
from the angularity
of their sound
like a mound
of dirt above
a mole's hole.

Pete's Dead

To Alene
It
flies on blue
and green
wings
from the chair
to the couch.
I shoot
a wooden arrow
with a rubber
tip
and strike
it dead.
Eros
weeps,
as we bury it
in a red
and black
matchbox
in the brown yard
behind the white
house

Message in a Bottle

The blue message
sealed
in a clear bottle
by a layer
of yellow beeswax
chewed slowly
in the green spring
unconceals
in black winter
the red shipwreck
to the gray other.

The Hermit

She found the hermit on the west beach looking for flotsam.
"Love me," she said. He turned slowly, answering her call,
not because he wanted to love her, that was not in his mind.
He turned because he thought he heard a gull
or a sea lion; those were the things he turned to see.
When he recognized her, he turned away
because the sea frothed white in a strong wind
and the sky masked a somber gray.

Her Spring Revolt

vowel revolution
leads to noun resolution

when word-scree
blocked the pass
I brought my spoon
and cereal bowl

and when word-shards
severed the Irish trail
I fetched my fork
and Austrian plate

but when I was late
you flew north
like a headless crow

with neither caw nor care

The Toad

The toad
squats
in black ooze
as the Nile
flows.
Empires
expire
and rot,
attracting green
flies
the toad spears
with a sticky
tongue.

Furnace Talk

To tap
the vein
requires
a pick
and ax,
a shovel
and a crowbar.
Dug-stone,
silent
as ore
out of the furnace,
sighs
sibilant
before the steam.

Chicago Lyre

desire
fuels
your blue flame

so do
not blame

the coal man
who fills
the gray bin

or the red brick
that warms
your face

likewise
do not harm
your faithful cow
that kicks the trace

instead embrace
the fire-threads
that embroider
green dreams
with yellow
word-shards
and the inner star
that singes
blue moons

The Shipwreck's Agenda

Ten years
from the day
of the shipwreck,
the shipwrecked
gleaned
a glimpse
of a gray sail
on green horizon.
As he cleared
his pale dwelling
of pink shells,
buried bottles,
sour weed
and fetid fish,
he brushed
away the vision
like a fly
near his ear
or an ant
on his leg.

Island Dwelling

Within the shipwrecked,
the island dwells.

Below clouds salt
a tremulous sky
and coral embraces
gastropods
as jungles
fringe
mountain roots.

Four-fold divinities
gibber like ghosts
on Pentecost
and flying fish
flutter
like ox tongues
on a hot griddle.

Insels

islands of ice

Electrical veins at night
silhouette brave borders
and slender shores. Stages
of yellow boards to play
the jester or the king,
while leviathans patrol
gulf streams and Catalinas
painted midnight-blue
hunt the darkness for Shelley's
monster preserved on a floe.

Freedom Is Between the Notes

poetry blooms on the paths of faery

Mr. and Mrs. Stevens select a black Steinway
for their sunroom in anticipation of summer.
Like a blackbird, it awaits the sirens
that sing operettas on the west side
between the ice-cream vendor from Venice
and the jeweler from Charleville.
After the thaw, silent summer arrives
and Mrs. Stevens takes a steam train alone
to the Poconos, and Mr. Stevens remains
in the city to advocate for the insureds
and play the piano. For seven hours straight
the first night he scratches the ivory keys,
like a snowcat against Orpheus's tree.
And so proceeds the solstice quotidian;
the infinitesimal gesture of their separation:
Mrs. Stevens golfs and Mr. Stevens plays.
Once, however, he pauses to erase a moist circle
left by his highball glass and Mrs. Stevens writes
requesting more money. He begrudgingly wires
her five dollars. On another day, he puzzles
out the latest Schoenberg and she buys
a dress. In August a rain falls on Manhattan
Island, and the water drains into the sea.
Most days though, Mr. Stevens pilots
a skiff between the keys of half-notes
that litter the green waters of the archipelago.

Anecdote of Psyche

No continents exist in the summer islands.
Instead the islands in-dwell in the castaway's gray iris,
where white sharks circle beneath a beached raft
that lists left in a lissome jolt with each azure wave
and parakeets with blue and green wings pinion a tattoo
at retreat toward a swiss-ed psyche. Landfall
stretches the comet's tail and a maître d' arrives
and recites French, while the barefoot castaway stands
on warm sand beside a chaise longue marked reserved.
In that internal archipelago a snowcat purrs
in an apple-barreled rum in the castaway's daiquiri,
informing him that the first island begets the second
and the second births the third, and the fourth
mirrors the first and the first awakens a fifth,
and there is no end nor order outside the rhythm
of the islands and no sound except the drone of a Hellcat,
scouting off the midway, and the pilot's hand vibrating on the stick
as icebergs calve from green glaciers in the north.

The Myth of the Snail

Each day it journeys
from the rose leaf
to the yard's loam
alone.
Without the help of any god,
it carries a shell
that grows evenly
through the years,
marking the limits
of its world.
Its boundary of being
measures the stretch of silver
between the rose leaf
and the grass blade.

Autobiography

Wolves run in the Schwarzwald,
while time ticks away.

Wolf-girls in dirndls
dance down wind
of the lone wolf.

The snail slides
along the frozen edge
of the fennel leaf
as the funicular
flees the flatland.

Wolf-girls follow
the scent
of the raven's wing
and light a candle
in Montmartre.

From Dali
he stole the snail
and from Jung
he followed the raven
to the wolf's door.
He lay on Freud's
couch for twelve years
and lived alone
in a world
grown dark.

Deutschland soured
the madness
in his blood
and left the cannibal
hungering for more,
as the wolf-girl
descended
into his shadow's
ruthless
solitude.

The Shipwreck's Dream

The shipwreck dreams of Abraham's sacrifice.
He awakens with a cough and these words:
"Abraham walks on the edge of his knife."
Meanwhile, the monkeys gambol in the palms;
the stream rushes to the sea;
snails flourish under red leaves;
and turtles lay eggs in the sand.
The night passes;
the moon wanes;
the mountain's gray silhouette
casts its shadows over the beach.

Pharos

Pharos
shines
on Ouroboros's tail
and greets
Caesar
in his biremes
and Cleopatra
in her rug.

Alexandria

The silver trout,
like a slender thread,
arrows
through an oblong eye
of a brass needle,
and threads
an Egyptian done
to a Greek's doing
beyond the edge
of a Roman sea.

Proper Study

Study
red fox
in winter
rather than Caliban,
and discover
what nature
in an unnatural
world
struggles
to be.

Die Vergangenheit

I enjoy *bonitas*
dancing the tango
but when I think
about the *petit pendant*
I know the *après durée*
is the proper place to play

-∞ space in self

in time

from right
to left

we turn
toward home

our advance
retreats
into self

a minor mirror
of nature's
preeminence

and negative
space

Sound Considered

Shipwreckt
sits
on the fringe
of the palms'
skirt
and ponders
the sense
and sound
of wind
and surf
surging
against
shore.

Will

Wolves hunt in packs
but they weary
of the long chase.
Others never tire.
Their will,
fueled by desire,
drives them on,
until their prey
falls helpless,
its heart
bursting
from the run.

Winter Hunts

Wolf-words weary elk-bulls
worrying them until they fall,
their hamstrings sprung,
their feet odd,
and their rhythm dead.
Ground squirrels sleep
silent under leaf and moss,
while bears birth cubs
in shallow caves
and snow blankets
the north face of a higher glen.
Inertia is the greenest god
draining words white.
Gasping glossolalia
surfeits all sentence sense
until the silver thread
of their dying sibilance
stretches as far back
as forward. Only fatigue
traps the line at full stop.
Only spring or hunger
wakes the hibernating beasts.

Philosophe Blanc

Roasted in winter
the blanched peanuts
attract the *philosophe blanc*,
a convivial recluse
who hunts book-trolls
and wolf-words.
His search is endless;
his trophies legion.
Each primordial word
trapped in his brass trap
provides flesh
of wet clay
to the silent god,
who becomes conscious
only in the white light
of the wolf-word's howl
or the book-troll's grunt.

Anecdote of the Center

In a Salon de Thé
in Algiers
a man in white
instructed the other:
take a linen
sheet of Egyptian
leaf
and draw a circle
in the center.
Fill it with graphite
from Pennsylvania.
Wait
for the world
to coalesce
around
its circumference.
Then blow
upon its borders
until it inflates
into a white sphere.
When the pressure
equalizes
balance
it like Chaplin's
globe;
rotate it,
do it,
until it holds.

Incarnation

The imagination
shines
from the center
and incarnates
Abel's flesh.
Through the circle
he knows
the circumference
and the roundness
of the jar.
From the forest
the unknown
vibrates black
and void;
while within
the sphere
sustains
all light.

Fox-clock

Fox-clock has no face,
no hands, no springs,
no gears. And yet, the fox
awakes with the morning sun,
hunts under the moon's mellow light,
dines on chickens, ducks, and eggs,
dozes in the forest's green shadow,
mates in the farmer's glen,
births in a shallow hidden den,
and dies without fear
or imminent dread
of its inevitable end.

Summer 1958

He shot a single round
into the silent wood
on a summer's eve.
The bullet smashed limbs
and something substantial fell
to the shadowed ground—
a great silhouette
shaded gray in the dusk.
He guessed it was a bird.
Night descended
and he thought
he heard weeping
in the woods.
He begged leave
to look
but it was late
and they refused.
The next morning
he searched
for spoor
but found nothing
but fallen limbs,
dead leaves,
and pine needles.
The darkness dressed
a dire drama;
the sun
defined
a summer's day.

The Net-Maker

He sits on the beach
of pebbled sand
and knits a net
to snare silver fish
scuttling in shoals
of the sullen sea.
Sometimes he snatches
a school of shining fish.
At others, a sea lion
shimmering black
in the moon's light
writhes in anguish
in the tangled threads
and he repents
and sets it free.

Matthew Arnold's Essay

When the doing fails and the Hebraic command
goes unheeded, my right hand quakes
and shivers from fear and I turn toward the other—
the Hellenic release, the sinister side—
and seek solace in the unreal.
The poem contains the not-doing
while alluding to the doing. The script,
a liquid sculpture, stains the page.
Arnold engineered the seesaw;
he saw the necessity in structure
balanced among the ancients. Stevens
picked it up like a fumbled ball
and ran with it, speaking its division
over and over in one guise or another.
He found release in the up and down strokes,
and threaded the needle with its theme,
like Crane and Carlyle before him,
the great Peripatetics.

La Ronde

From the fire comes the shadow.
From the shadow comes the silhouette.
From the silhouette comes the story.
From the story comes the tale.
From the tale comes the myth.
From the myth comes the gods.
From the gods comes man.
From man comes the fire.

Seeking Celan 1968

The gray stone absorbs
her black lace as silver flakes fall
on the cobblestones near the museum.
Her perfumed thighs
spread by his warm fingers
define the degree
of their digression toward the word
defined against polished phrases
reflected from Venetian glass.
Its sound like a laurel leaf
caught in the fall breeze
soars above a serpentine Seine.
Beginning at La Manche
it arrests itself
beneath the bridge
of his mounting distress.

Icarus's Lament

At the journey's end
he awoke to find
a pile of feathers
beneath his perch.
The heat
of the summer
solstice
melted the wax
that secured
his ivory pinions,
freeing the crow
feathers
to fall
like frozen flakes
in winter.
Thus his childhood
ended with a failed
experience
of flight.
Days of toil
stretched before him.
Ravens laugh
and crows caw
their ridicule.

Rose + Snail

the quotidian
is today
and tomorrow
until the end

the end
is no concern
of the snail's
or mine

our task
is to struggle
to the center
of the rose
or breath
at the end
of the line

breath-signs
signal signatures
signed

only then
will done
be
done
and words
sealed

Infinite Bees

what do
I do
when doing
does
nothing

note
nothing
today
produces
no honey
tomorrow

but

you say

one bee
working
finitely
finishes
an infinite
honey

drop

Kavka/Jackdaw

The jackdaw,
born Kavka
in Prague,
fractures
a semiotic
chirp
that sounds
Latin
not Greek
and festers
black
like a chow's
tongue.

A Sunday Fight Ends Now

now

we have
now

and
the memory
of the not now

the next now
is not yet now
and maybe
never will be

our now
continues
until there is no now

a point
marked
posthumously
as the final

now

Death Visits Kilgore on Sunday

deadness
surrounds us

interrupts us
from our rounds

nestled
in nests

it flies
in our face

surprising us
even though

we knew
it was there

waiting

now
and for ever

Anecdote of a Black Chow

The black chow
was his last dog.
No more dogs
to love; its memory
lives in his sadness.
A vestigial dog
haunts his stoop.
Its bark wakes him
from an afternoon nap.
He finds stiff
black hairs
on splintered
hooks splitting
away from the frame
of the screen door.
He senses its body
in the shadowed room;
he smells its oily pelt.
Its black tongue
lolls from its snout
at dusk
when the snails
cross the sidewalk
to the rose garden.